EARTH
The Water Planet

Greg Roza

Rosen Classroom Books & Materials™
New York

Published in 2006 by The Rosen Publishing Group, Inc.
29 East 21st Street, New York, NY 10010

Book Design: Jennifer Crilly

Photo Credits: Cover, p. 1 © Robert Holmes/Corbis; p. 5 © PhotoDisc; p. 6 © Mark Chivers/Getty Images; p. 9 © Anne Ackermann/Getty Images; p. 10 © Macduff Everton/Corbis; p. 13 © Peter Essick/Getty Images; p. 14 © Steve Kaufman/Corbis; p. 17 by Jennifer Crilly; p. 18 © Naruaki Onishi/Getty Images; p. 20 © Charles & Josette Lenars/Corbis

ISBN: 1-4042-5827-2
6-pack ISBN: 1-4042-5828-0

Manufactured in the United States of America

Contents

The Water Planet

We live on planet Earth. Earth is one of nine planets in our solar system. Scientists think that the solar system formed about 4.6 billion years ago as a cloud of gases and dust. This cloud began to spin and fall in on itself. Over time, this caused the sun to form. The planets formed soon after.

Earth is special. It is the only planet in the solar system with a plentiful supply of water. It is also the only planet that has life as we know it.

More than two-thirds of Earth's surface is covered with water. This is why it looks blue from outer space.

Where Did Earth's Water Come From?

When Earth formed, scientists think that it was a dry lump of solid rock. This lump of rock had trapped many elements, including the gases **oxygen** and **hydrogen**. As Earth spun, some matter moved to the center of Earth and some moved to the surface. This released hydrogen and oxygen into the space around Earth. These and other gases formed the air around Earth. It also allowed the oxygen and hydrogen to join and form water.

Earth's surface was very hot when water first formed. Rain boiled off this hot surface turning into water vapor. As more water formed, Earth's surface cooled. Earth's rain eventually formed oceans.

Life on Earth

Scientists know that life began on Earth about 3.5 billion years ago, but they are not sure how it happened. Many scientists think that life originated when **chemicals** in the oceans joined together with the aid of sunlight to form new chemicals. The new chemicals formed the types of matter that are found in all living creatures today.

Living things need water to carry out the processes that keep them alive. Human beings are about 65 percent water. Some living things, such as the tomato, can be as much as 95 percent water.

Doctors and scientists advise that we drink about eight glasses of water a day to stay healthy. Much of the water in our bodies comes from foods we eat.

Reservoirs

A **reservoir** is a place where a large amount of water gathers or is stored. Natural reservoirs include oceans, lakes, rivers, and streams. Earth's **ice caps** and icebergs are also natural reservoirs.

The oceans hold about 97.2 percent of all the water on Earth. Only about 2.8 percent of the water on Earth is freshwater. The ice caps and icebergs contain about 2 percent of the water on Earth. The other .8 percent can be found in the ground, in lakes, seas, rivers, and in the atmosphere.

More than two-thirds of Earth's freshwater is stored as ice. Most of this ice can be found in Earth's ice caps.

Wet Earth, Dry Earth

Some parts of Earth's surface have more water than others. The Amazon rain forest in South America is one of the wettest places on Earth. It receives more than 100 inches of rain a year. Because of this, the Amazon rain forest is home to the most types of plants and animals found anywhere in the world.

Few creatures can live in areas of the world where there is little water, like the Sahara Desert in Africa. The Sahara receives less than four inches of rain a year.

Some plants and animals have developed ways to live in very dry areas. Cacti, for example, are plants that can store water for when they need it. Many cacti also have very long roots that can reach water deep below the surface.

States of Water

Water can exist in three states depending on how hot or cold it is. At room **temperature** water is a liquid, which is something that takes the shape of the container holding it. When water is cold enough, it turns to ice, which is a solid. A solid is something that takes a specific shape and can be held in the hand.

When water is heated enough it boils. Boiling water turns into a gas called water vapor. Most gases have no shape or color.

On a snow (solid) covered mountain, water vapor (gas) rises off the hot springs (liquid) where a monkey is bathing. This monkey is experiencing water in all its forms.

The Water Cycle

Water on Earth is always changing.
Water in oceans, lakes, the ground, and
even in living things changes into a gas and
rises into the air. Once there, it forms clouds.
The water changes into rain or snow and
falls back to Earth. Much of this water falls
directly into bodies of water. Some rain
soaks the ground and is used by plants.
Some of the water runs off into bodies of
water. From there, the process starts all
over again. This process is known as the
water cycle.

Earth's water today is the same as it was millions of
years ago. The water in the water cycle has always been
there, and no new water ever joins it.

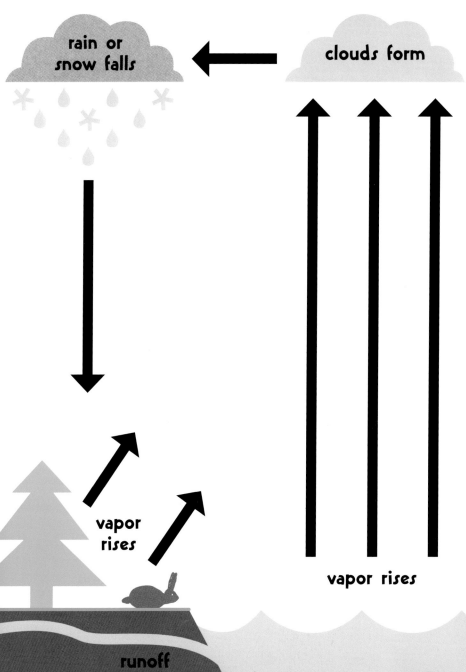

rain or snow falls

clouds form

vapor rises

vapor rises

runoff

17

The Properties of Water

Water is a universal solvent. This means that it can break down nearly every substance. Water has a high heat capacity, in other words it is able to take in a large amount of heat while its own temperature only rises slightly.

Water is made up of very tiny parts called **molecules**. These molecules cling to each other tightly. Because of this property water is able to creep up the stem of a plant.

Water molecules cling to each other tightly, creating sort of a skin on top of the water. This allows some insects to walk on the surface of calm water.

The Power of Water

Water can act with great force to change Earth's surface. When water hits or rushes over land, it can shape the way the land looks. Over time, rivers cut paths through solid rock. They carry tiny pieces of rock, soil, and sand with them. These pieces are deposited at the ends of rivers, creating new areas of land called deltas. Deltas are usually perfect for farming.

When too much rainwater or melting snow enters a river, the river can overflow and flood the area around it. Running water can also cause **erosion** to occur.

Mudslides occur when the soil on a hill or mountain contains too much water. This loosens the soil so much that it forms a wall of mud that can slide down the hill.

Water and Civilization

All **civilizations** depend on freshwater. The world's first civilizations appeared between the Tigris and the Euphrates rivers in the area that is today known as Iraq. Today, we depend on water for many uses. Not only do our bodies need water to live, but we also use it to farm, make power, travel on, and play in. Water is so important to us that we need to be careful not to pollute it. Polluted water is not safe to drink and takes a long time to clean itself.

Glossary

chemicals   Substances that can be mixed with other substances to cause reactions.

civilizations   Groups of people living in organized and similar ways.

erosion   The wearing away of land over time.

hydrogen   A colorless and odorless gas.

ice caps   Snow and ice covering areas of Earth.

molecules   Tiny building blocks that make up matter.

oxygen   A colorless gas that many forms of life need to live.

reservoir   A place where large amounts of water are stored.

temperature   How hot or cold something is.

water cycle   The process by which water evaporates from plants, animals, and bodies of water, and returns as rain and snow.

Index